E-COLLAR TRAINING FOR PET DOGS

THE ONLY RESOURCE YOU'LL NEED TO TRAIN YOUR DOG WITH THE AID OF AN ELECTRIC COLLAR

TED EFTHYMIADIS

E-collar Training For Pet Dogs

The only resource you'll need to train your dog with the aid of an electric training collar

Published by Ted Efthymiadis
Halifax NS Canada
www.tedsbooks.com

INTRODUCTION

It was 3 a.m. as I turned on my computer to sign onto a dog training internet forum. I went straight to the messages tab to see if he had sent me a reply. Here I was, a young man in Canada, waking in the middle of the night in the hope that I could touch base with a man named Jim who lived halfway around the world. Jim was a police K9 handler in Australia, and he had the answers that I needed to help Phoenix, my rescue dog.

Phoenix was my first dog. When I adopted him, I knew nothing about dogs, but to my credit, I was committed for the long haul. In the house, Phoenix was the perfect dog, but when he got outside all bets were off. My back pain started the moment I opened the front door; it was like watching a team of huskies pull a sled. The off leash experience was comparable in discomfort. Given that you're reading this book, you can likely sympathize with my issues.

"He needs to burn off his energy," I would tell myself as I let him off leash in the woods or "There's no one around, he'll be fine." Well that all changed the day of the raccoon incident. It was about 7:30 a.m. when we found ourselves in our daily plot of forest that was free of people and dogs. As I un-clipped his leash, I said a prayer as I did every day before letting him off leash. The first five minutes went well, he came every time I called his name, and the treats seemed to be effective and motivating. Then I heard it, screaming. If you've never heard the sound of a raccoon fighting for its life, I'll spare you the details. I ran as fast as I could toward the screaming. In what seemed like 15 seconds, Phoenix had its stomach ripped open. There was blood everywhere. The raccoon was still fighting back despite its intestines being outside of its body. Waiting for an opportune time, I grabbed his collar and hauled him off of the raccoon. Rest in peace, raccoon. I'm sorry I let you down.

The raccoon is a robust animal that can weigh up to thirty-five pounds. If Phoenix could tell his friends about the raccoon, he probably would have said it was at least sixty pounds, but I was there, it was more like twenty-five to thirty pounds. Wikipedia says the word raccoon comes from the Algonquin word arouhgcoune which translates to "he who scratches with his hands." The Algonquin clearly know what they are talking about because this raccoon had put up a serious fight. Phoenix was bleeding from his face, and his ear was torn pretty badly.

I'm ashamed of this story, but I tell it to illustrate two points.

- Well-meaning people can give their dogs freedom they've not earned.
- There is hope despite what your dog is like now.

That very day I decided that enough was enough, I could no longer let my dog act like a predator. Either I would have to keep him on a leash for the rest of his life or I would have to break down and buy an e-collar. After a few weeks of keeping him exclusively on a leash, I decided to invest the money into a good quality e-collar so that Phoenix could have some freedom to run off leash. In those days, e-collars were rather primitive and utilitarian, but I knew it was my only hope for Phoenix to have off leash freedom again.

Phoenix and I had already done plenty of positive training, but the results were mixed. When I had his favorite treats, he was responsive 99% of the time. As you can imagine, my issue began when he saw or smelled something he wanted to kill and then all bets were off. We started our e-collar training by following some step by step instructions, focusing on what is called a "crittering protocol." The crittering protocol was somewhat effective but didn't seem to get to the root of the issue, it was more of a band-aid solution. That's when I connected with Jim.

As mentioned earlier, Jim was a Police K9 handler in Australia who had experience training police dogs with the aid of e-collars. E-collar education in those days was hard to come by, and e-collar resources for behavioral issues were almost impossible to find. Jim was nice enough to help me over private message on a dog training forum we were both a part of. He was straight to the point and didn't hide anything which was exactly what I needed to hear. Despite his "shoot from the hip" teaching style, he had a wit and vocabulary that only an Australian could have. I was never able to meet Jim in person, but I like to think he was an extra in *Crocodile Dundee*.

If you're reading this book, you probably own a dog you're having issues with and I can definitely sympathize with that. I started out just like you, and now I'm a professional trainer who travels around the world teaching dog owners and dog trainers how to live a more fulfilling life with their dogs. People turn to me when they are convinced they have tried everything. In this book, I'll share with you what I've learned from some of the worlds best e-collar trainers and what I've learned in more than ten thousand hours training dogs with the aid of e-collars.

Phoenix went on to live with three different cats without any aggression, and of course became the inspiration in my decision to become a professional dog trainer. Some look at dogs like Phoenix as a curse; I look at them as a blessing because without him I never would have become a dog trainer. Had I adopted an easy-going golden retriever you would not be reading this book right now. *We tend to get the dogs we need, not the dogs we want.*

The benefits of e-collar training

Not since the invention of the leash has the world of dog training seen such an all-around training tool for dogs. The e-collar is most known for its ability to communicate with and correct a dog at a distance. However, this is just the start. Here's a list of areas where the e-collar can be used with great results.

- Recall (coming when called)
- Resource guarding
- Perimeter training
- Pulling on the leash
- Human/dog aggression
- Jumping on people
- Excessive barking
- Hunting dog applications
- Stealing food from the counter
- Eating feces

The e-collar shines as a method of communication and correction that does not erode the trust and relationship that a client and dog have built. Things like strong leash corrections or yelling at your dog can deteriorate the relationship that you've formed with your dog and are to be avoided at all costs. If you're frustrated with your dog, don't worry because all of my clients are feeling overwhelmed the day that we start training. This tool will aid you in being able to stay calm during the training process, without making it personal when your dog does something that you disapprove of.

Another benefit of e-collar training is that you'll have the leverage to communicate with and correct your dog at a distance like never before. This is a huge deal and will completely change the way your dog thinks about trying to get away with bad things when they are far enough away from you and you can't do anything at the moment. Most e-collars are fully waterproof, which is great for dogs who go outside in the rain or for dogs who love to swim, but keep in mind that e-collar stimulation becomes less effective in the water, rather than being more intense. You will find that about a quarter of the power of your e-collar will dissipate into the water.

What are the potential risks of e-collar training?

If you purchase the right tool and use it properly, e-collar training has zero risks associated with it. Unfortunately, some dog owners buy them without any education, and people should always follow a step by step plan if they want to properly use this tool. Many dog owners see them as a quick fix, and that couldn't be further from the truth. As you'll uncover as you read further into this book, e-collar training is not a quick fix. It takes hours of training to do this work flawlessly, but the time investment will allow you to accomplish things you never thought possible.

The EZ900 from e-collar technologies is hands down the best e-collar unit available for pet dog applications

TOOLS

*T*he *Electric collar*
              In life, one should not attempt to save money on 4 things.

- Q-tips
- Birth control
- E-collars
- A child's car seat

WITH THE TREMENDOUS growth of online marketplaces, the sheer number of e-collars the average dog owner can buy is astounding. If you've yet to buy an e-collar, think long and hard about this decision before you invest money into something that may turn out to be utterly useless. I can't stress how important it is to purchase a quality e-collar. Certainly all e-collars are not made equally. Let's explore some of the options you'll want to navigate before buying your e-collar, and read along if you already own an e-collar to be sure that you have the right model for your dog. Personally, I only use E-collar

Technologies products, but you can also find good options from Dogtra and a few other notable brands.

YOU MIGHT BE TEMPTED to cut corners an d buy a cheap knock-off that's made in China that has one hundred levels, and I would discourage you from doing that. Trust me when I say you get what you pay for. E-collars you can buy in most big box stores are also rarely going to be what you want to buy. If you don't buy from a reputable company, you won't have access to aftermarket accessories like different contact points, replacement batteries, repairs, and you will likely not have a warranty. If you can't change the contact points on your e-collar and own a thick-haired dog, you may as well throw your e-collar in the garbage because it will not work on your dog.

LEVEL SELECTION

I highly recommend only training your dog with an e-collar that has one hundred or more levels of intensity. Without a large selection of levels to choose from your training will prove to be overbearing. The only two high-quality brands who sell e-collars capable of one hundred levels are E-collar Technologies and Dogtra. Other notable brands who have shown a long history of producing well-made, reliable e-collars are Sportdog, DT Systems, Garmin, Tritronics. However, I don't suggest these e-collars as they don't have the flexibility of one hundred levels or more. You can do e-collar training with fewer level selections, but I do not recommend it. Training with e-collars that have six or even sixteen levels is like trying to ride a bike cross country on a single speed bike. Sure it can be done, but I would much rather take that journey on a bike with more gearing options. Some dogs are very sensitive to the e-collar stimulation, and if your e-collar only has 6 levels you will quickly find the e-collar to be too intense for those dogs. Level 1/6 may be too low, and 2/6 may be too high.

. . .

TONE OR VIBRATE

Many e-collars are capable of emitting an audible tone or a collar vibration. We'll discuss these features in later chapters, but you can do training without either option. The vibration feature is not typically something I use with clients, but the tone can be a great benefit during the training process. Most e-collar units don't have both tone and vibrate, so I would generally suggest purchasing an e-collar with tone rather than vibrate if you have the option.

DISTANCE

A quarter mile is the absolute minimum that you'll want in an e-collar. Half mile is the standard for high-quality e-collars.

¼ mile = 1320 feet, 402 meters, 440 yards
½ mile = 2640 feet, 804 meters, 880 yards
¾ mile = 3960 feet, 1207 meters, 1320 yards
1 mile = 5280 feet, 1609 meters, 1760 yards

POWER OUTPUT

A common misconception about e-collars is that the size of your dog will determine what level they will work with on the e-collar. I've trained hundreds of dogs that weighed more than one hundred pounds, and many of them worked at low levels. I've also seen some small dogs that worked at much higher levels.

AS A GENERAL RULE, e-collars come in two output formats: low-medium and high-extra. Take the E-collar Technologies model mini 300 for example. It's rated as a low-medium output model and is a great choice for small and medium sized dogs. The Dogtra 280C is also a good option for small and medium sized dogs. Keep in mind that even though many big dogs can be worked at relatively low e-collar levels, some dogs who have high prey drives (the strong urge to chase) can disregard the low-medium output e-collars when they are in a predatory mode. It's for this reason that I suggest high-extra output e-collars like the Dogtra 1900S or the E-collar Technologies ET-800 for dogs over fifty pounds who have a history of aggression or have a propensity to chase animals. Bear in mind that the high-extra output models have one hundred or more levels so they can still be used just as subtly as the low-medium models previously suggested. This extra output will likely never be used on your dog, but it's nice to know that it's there in case you need it. Unfortunately, you will not know if you need the extra output until at least three weeks into the training process, so buying a low-medium output model might be a waste of money if your dog needs a higher output model.

EXPANDING *for multiple dog households*

Most e-collar manufacturers offer e-collars that are expandable for multiple dog households. Some are sold as single dog units that have the capability to add an additional receiver and others come in the box as 2,3, or 4 dog units. Many of my clients decide to get another dog after our training is done and they love the ability to expand their e-collar when they open their hearts and homes to a new dog. If you're considering getting another dog in the future it may be advisable to buy an e-collar that has the capacity to expand. When training multiple dogs with an e-collar, I highly suggest that you train each dog separately until both dogs are doing extremely well before working with two or more dogs at the same time. Remember that e-collars are designed to only deliver stimulation to one collar at a time which means you cannot press two or more stimulation buttons at the same time because the radio frequency will block both signals. In the event that both of your dogs are running away from you and you need to call them both back at the same time, you'll need to correct the dog who is leading the chase and then tap the other if applicable. If you are using the e-collar because you have a multiple dog home and your dogs are fighting, I highly recommend bringing in a professional dog trainer who can help you with this extremely advanced issue because it's very dangerous and if not done perfectly the outcome could be catastrophic. In the event that you bring in a qualified trainer and you are using the e-collar, you will want to purchase two separate e-collars in the event that both dogs need to be corrected at the same time.

Purchasing an e-collar from a reputable company like E-collar Technologies will give you the ability to have long-lasting recharge-able batteries and purchase different collar styles. Most important you'll have access to a variety of contact points. Buying an e-collar that has rechargeable batteries is a must. Some lower-priced options are powered by batteries that you need to replace on an almost daily basis. Often, these batteries are specialty batteries that you can't buy at local stores. It can't be overstated how much extra money these e-collar units will cost you over the long-term, so they are to be avoided at all cost. A quality e-collar unit will have rechargeable batteries in both the remote and the collar.

BUNGEE COLLARS ARE a fabulous upgrade that you can buy for the majority of e-collars and allow the collar to stretch. 100% of e-collars will either use a ¾ inch or 1-inch width collar so it's easy to find bungee collars for any e-collar. Your dog's neck will increase in size slightly as your dog's temperature rises from exercise. These collars also make putting on your e-collar fast and easy while still providing a proper snug fit.

HAVING access to several different contact points for your dog is essential to consistent e-collar training. Over the years I've had count-less dog owners come in asking for help with their dog who were convinced that their dog had such a high pain threshold that they would not feel the e-collar. This is not the case, and it's always a contact point issue that can be easily solved if you own a quality e-collar with different contact points for dogs with short, medium, long, and extra-thick coats. With short-medium haired dogs you'll probably be fine with the stock contact points that come with your e-collar out of the box.

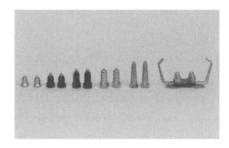

From left to right: short, medium, long, thick coat, extra long coat, extreme wings

Short contact points can be a great option for bully breed dogs, bull terriers, french bulldogs, english bulldogs, boxers, great danes, and some hunting dogs with short coats like vizslas and weimaraners. I use the medium on breeds like goldendoodles, labrador retrievers, border collies, and most mixed breeds. Long contact points are a great option for german shepherds, rottweilers, golden retrievers, and portuguese water dogs. Thick coat contact are used on akitas, bernese mountain dogs, great pyrenees, and even some german shepherds with extra dense undercoats. Extra long coat is a good option for newfoundland dogs and grizzly bears. Extreme wings are also a good solution for thick coated dogs and dog with extra long coats. Most e-collar contact points are made out of surgical grade stainless steel which prevents corrosion and rust even in salt water conditions. If it appears that your dog's neck is irritated by the e-collar be sure that the contact points are made of stainless steel; if they are and you're still having issues, you should purchase a pair of hypoallergenic contact points that are made out of titanium. This issue is extremely rare, but some dogs are allergic to the small amount of Nickel (5%) in the stainless steel.

· · ·

FITTING *the e-collar*

The two most common mistakes dog owners make when starting e-collar training are not using the proper e-collar contact points and not fitting the e-collar appropriately. The stimulation that the e-collar delivers feels similar to a Tens unit commonly used by physiotherapists and chiropractors for muscle rehabilitation. If your e-collar is not getting good contact with your dog's muscle, the stimulation will be inconsistent.

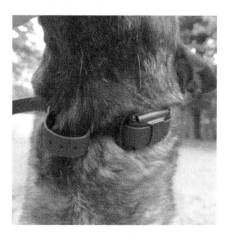

PROPER PLACEMENT *of the e-collar on BB's neck*

ANOTHER COMMON MISTAKE is to put the collar too low on your dog's neck; this is not advised since most dogs necks are shaped like a traffic cone. They are bigger at the base then they are at the top. If you place the e-collar at the base of the neck, as your dog is playing around outside the collar will work its way up your dog's neck and will no longer have a snug fit. A good frame of reference is to cinch the collar down so that you are able to slip two of your fingers underneath the collar strap on the back of your dog's neck.

HERE IS a recap of how to fit the e-collar properly.

- Be sure that you have the correct contact points on your e-collar
- De-shed your dog's neck if they have a thick coat
- Place the e-collar high on your dog's neck
- Do not place on the top of your dog's neck, the left or right sides are fine
- Tighten to a snug fit, use two fingers to gauge the fit
- Be sure to rotate the e-collar every 2 hours of use to prevent any irritation
- Do not attach a leash to the e-collar

WE NEVER ATTACH **a leash to the e-collar**. Martingale collars are a great collar that we often use during training. They are inexpensive to purchase and can be commonly found at any pet store. Any collar or harness that you want to use to attach your leash is fine. However, they must be the proper size for your dog and tightly fitted to your dog's neck. A martingale collar tightens if a dog tries to back out of the collar which is why it's the collar of choice for many dog trainers.

If your dog can back out of his collar, you'll need to get a martingale collar to eliminate the chance of this happening during the training process.

SAFETY

If you ever allow your dog to wear the e-collar for more than a few hours you'll want to rotate the collar to another part of your dog's neck. Some dogs' necks are perfectly fine with the e-collar for long periods and others are more sensitive. But as a rule I suggest to rotate after 2 hours of wearing the e-collar. Also, as a general rule, if your dog swims you'll want to take the e-collar off and allow their necks to dry before putting the collar back on and be sure to wash the e-collar in warm soapy water.

CHECK out your (2) free step by step e-collar training video series at www.tedsbooks.com/watch

OFF LEASH TRAINING

$\mathcal{B}$efore transitioning off leash every dog owner needs to teach the four pillars.

- Where the stimulation is coming from
- How to turn on the stimulation
- How to turn off the stimulation
- How to avoid the stimulation

ALL TOO OFTEN, I hear of well-meaning dog owners who rush the e-collar training process without doing the foundation training properly. Rushing this process may seem like a viable option but trust me when I say that it's going to be a bad decision over the long term. Owners that rush this process are almost always incredibly frustrated with their dogs and feel as if they can't wait any longer. It will be tempting to skip some things as we progress, but let's do right by your dog and remember that this training is not just for your dog but also for you.

. . .

FOR THE FIRST THREE DAYS, you'll be doing just two quick sessions per day: one in the morning and one in the evening, inside your home or apartment. Your lessons are to be no more than five minutes. Yes, you read that correctly. If your dog has a strong desire to eat his/her dog food you can use their meals for training. If this is the case, give your dog a small handful of food each repetition during your training sessions until you are done with the meal. If you feel that treats are going to be a better motivation, you can use those. Dehydrated beef liver treats are always a favorite with clients' dogs and they are low in calories.

FIRST, we'll need to determine what method you will use to prompt for your dog's attention with the e-collar, the tone or the vibration. When we progress off leash and work at long distances, this step will prove to be of benefit and will be paired with your recall command (come). The method of prompting will typically depend on your e-collar manufacturer and model. If you have an e-collar that is capable of giving an audible tone you will use the tone, if your e-collar has a vibration we'll use that. If your e-collar has both options I would highly suggest using the tone because I have seen dogs that quickly become afraid of the vibrate setting. There is something about the vibration that can scare some dogs and so if you are going to use it be sure to only use it outside with lots of distraction for the first session which will decrease the likelihood of your dog being scared of it. If your collar does not have a tone or vibrate, you can use a come command instead. The tone/vibration will be referred to as T/V as we progress in this book.

YOU CAN START by turning on your e-collar and remote and fitting the collar on your dog's neck. You'll begin inside the house with a regular six to eight foot leash on your dog. Say come and tap the T/V button as you walk away from your dog. Say Yes and give them food/treat and praise when your dog comes to you. You should notice your dog following you around the room and that's ok, just walk backwards. If they are already walking toward you, you can still give them the commands and tap the T/V button. This is actually a good thing to see, think of it like an employee who's arriving for a work shift early. You'll do this for five minutes and then end the session. If your dog seems slightly perplexed by the tone/vibrate, help them by calling them with their favorite nickname, giving them some praise. Don't be afraid to shower your dog with praise when they come to you. Holding a treat in your hand as you call them can also help, don't be afraid to look silly when you do this because you want your dog to think the T/V is something that brings good things.

WHAT THESE LESSONS ARE TEACHING:

- Come and T/V are coming from you
- Come and T/V are essentially the same command
- Yes means good things are coming

It's essential that you only use the e-collar for these lessons for the first 1-3 days.

FOR DAYS 3-7 you'll be doing just two quick sessions per day. One in the morning and one in the evening, these lessons will be done outside in your yard or on your leash walks. Your lessons are to be no more than five to seven minutes. It's no longer required to do your lessons from days 1-3. What you are teaching in the next few days will cover many different teaching points that will prepare your dog for the off leash control that's soon to come. It will also teach your dog all four of the pillars of e-collar training. Where the stimulation is coming from, how to turn on the stimulation, how to turn off the stimulation, and how to avoid the stimulation.

. . .

You'll need to start each lesson by finding your dog's e-collar working level. Think of the working level as the lowest level your dog will feel and show you a slight response that they are feeling the stimulation. You can find your own e-collar working level by placing the e-collar on your hand, starting at level one giving the button a tap and increase one level at a time until you feel a slight tingle in your hand. That's your e-collar working level. Take your time during this step. Keep in mind that your e-collar should be using the continuous stimulation mode when finding the e-collar working level. Continuous stimulation means that when you tap the button it gives just a quick stimulation, but if you hold the button down it will give continuous stimulation until you release the button. More on that in future lessons.

Finding the initial e-collar level

There are dozens of behaviors that dogs will show when they start to feel the e-collar stimulation. The most common response is to see your dog looking around like a bug just landed of their neck or head. Other dogs will just stop what they are doing and look a little bit confused. Some dogs will not show you a behavioral change but you will spot a little muscle twitch on your dog's neck. This is most common with bully breeds as they have very muscular necks and short coats. Others will show even more subtle signs like quickly licking their lips. Think of it like this, if you were walking down a busy street in your town or city and someone tapped you on the shoulder from behind and then disappeared, what would you do? You would likely look around with a confused look on your face. This is the typical response we see with most dogs.

Start at level 1/100, tap the continuous button once quickly and watch for a slight change in your dog's behavior. Continue by going up to level 2, tapping once, then going to level 3 and so on until your dog shows one of the subtle responses listed above. When you've found that level, this is the level we will start our lesson at. The key to finding the right e-collar working level is to give yourself time to find it. The first time I do this with each dog I typically will take four to five minutes just to find the right level. If you find yourself going over 20/100 it's very likely that your e-collar is not getting proper contact on your dog's neck and you'll want to turn the level back down to zero, and tighten the strap and start again or change the contact points that came with your e-collar. Each e-collar is different, of course, as is each dog, so it's hard to give a general level that your dog will work at. I've seen dogs feel as low as a level 1/100 which for me is inconceivable because I feel a level 12/100 on my neck with most e-collars that I have used. Never assume that your dog is going to work high on the e-collar until training proves that point. If your dog is visibly uncomfortable when you press the continuous button, the level is too high, the response should be incredibly subtle.

START WALKING your dog in the yard or on the sidewalk outside of your house. The moment your dog gets fixated on something in front of you and starts to get close to the end of the leash you should stop, say come and tap the T/V button. If they look a little confused you'll want to encourage your dog to come to you and walk away while enticing them with a treat. Be sure to give your dog some food/treats and some praise when they come in your direction.

YOU MIGHT FIND that your dog is too distracted by the sights and smells of the outdoors and so you'll need to tap the continuous stimulation button at the level we just found to be the e-collar working level.

THE MOMENT your dog gets fixated on something in front of you and starts to get close to the end of the leash you should stop, say come and tap the T/V button, If your dog doesn't change directions and come with you right away, hold down the continuous button for about one to two seconds and walk in the opposite direction. You can give food/treat or praise regardless of how your dog does. Continue to practice this for five to seven minutes, and you're done until your next session. Your dog should quickly learn that they can avoid the e-collar stimulation by focusing on turning when you turn. This simple exercise teaches a few concepts we'll need later in training.

As you progress in your training lessons you may find the need to increase the e-collar stimulation level, this is very common. Increase your level one level at a time until you start to see your dog becoming more focused on turning when you turn. If your dog turns with you, you do not need to press the continuous button.

What these lessons are teaching:

- The tone/vibrate/e-collar stimulation is coming from you.
- Ignoring our come command turns on the stimulation.
- Following our come command will turn off the stimulation.
- Your dog can avoid the subtle e-collar stimulation by making turns with you.

If you are doing these lessons in your yard, I suggest walking in straight lines and making tight 180 degree turns. If you are doing these lessons on your walks, you'll do a 180 degree turn on the sidewalk and then add another 180 turn so that you can continue with your walk. These sessions will also help your dog slow down while walking if they love to pull you down the road.

For days 7-12 You will be working on essentially the same homework that you focused on in days 3-7 however your recalls will become increasingly difficult by incrementally adding more distance and distraction. You'll use a long leash for your homework, fifteen to twenty-five feet is ideal. If the end goal is to have your dog off leash they will need to pass some tests before you can be sure that you'll have the control you desire when going off leash. These sessions will be done outside. You can increase the session time to ten to thirty minutes as desired, again two sessions each day.

BE sure to properly fit your dog's e-collar, turn it on, attach your long leash and have food/treats ready. Start your dog out with an easy lesson by putting some hotdogs or cheese out in your yard before your session when your dog is inside. You can do this just the same if you live in a busy city by planting some hotdogs in places your dog will be able to see and smell when you take them out. Plant four to five hotdogs in different areas, then take your dog out for a walk and allow your dog to smell the hotdogs but don't allow them enough room on the long leash to get to them. Start by finding your dogs working e-collar level. Say come and tap the T/V button, if they don't come toward you right away, hold down the continuous button for about 1-2 seconds and walk in the opposite direction. You can give food/treat or praise regardless of when your dog comes to you. You might find that your dog ignores the first come command and T/V and then also ignores the continuous button, if that's the case, increase your e-collar level gradually until your dog avoids the hotdogs and starts walking with you. Shower them with praise and give them food/treats when they come back to you. Move onto the next hotdog distraction and do the same thing. Continue to practice this for 15-30 minutes setting up 4-5 hotdog distractions and you're done until your next session. Your dog should quickly learn that they can avoid the e-collar stimulation by focusing on coming to you when they hear the Tone or feel the Vibrate. To that point, they will also be given praise and something tasty if they come to you.

IF YOU FIND that your dog comes nicely with a level 10/100 with little distraction but need to increase to a level 15 or 20/100 to follow you when the hotdogs are out that's normal. Your dog might need to be increased 1 extra level, or dozens of levels, you won't know until you try. If you know that after setting up the hotdog distraction you need to increase to 20/100 every time, you can start to assume that level in the future by increasing your level in anticipation, I call this pattern levels.

PATTERN LEVELS

Every client will notice pattern levels, some dogs will need slight increases and others will need bigger jumps in the levels depending on the distraction. The important part is to remember that you need to take the time to figure out these pattern levels, never assuming too quickly. Please take care to remember to turn your e-collar level down after a higher pattern level. I use an E-collar Technologies pro educator on my Labrador retriever when we are doing retriever work in the water because she likes to cheat and retrieve the closest retrieve instead of the one I tell her to retrieve. When she's in the water the e-collar stimulation is going to be less intense than if she was not swimming and she's very driven when she's working so her pattern level jumps from a 16/100 regular working level to a 30/100 every time. Look for patterns in your dog's levels as you train.

WHY IT's ok to give multiple commands

Have you ever heard a dog trainer say "You never repeat a command because then your dogs will learn to ignore you?" This phrase is common among trainers who don't use e-collars. It's absolutely correct for those who are not using an e-collar, but completely false in regards to clients and trainers who are using e-collars. Giving multiple commands can actually produce a dog who comes to you much quicker because of the way commands are reinforced.

- The first command is easy and rewarding
- The second command is annoying and rewarding
- The third command is uncomfortable and rewarding

THE FIRST COMMAND is easy because they avoid any potential correction and are rewarded for coming. The second command is annoying by adding a low level continuous e-collar stimulation and then rewarding when your dog comes to you. The third command is uncomfortable when your dog is clearly ignoring two commands they hear or feel and they are still rewarded when they come to you. So why do I give food/treats or praise every time during the training phase? Because I want my dog to expect good things when they come back to me. Never get angry with your dog even if they didn't come perfectly like you had expected. If you were a dog, you would be less likely to come if you knew your owner was mad at you. You want your dog to rush back to you like a kid running downstairs on Christmas morning.

FOR DAYS 12-18. Off leash training should always start on a regular length leash, then transition to your long leash, then dropping the long leash, and finally removing it completely. At this stage in training, you should have much more control over your dog while out on walks, in your yard, and at the park but you'll still be confined to your long leash. You can make your final transitions to off leash freedom over the next few days using two different training protocols.

YOU'LL WANT to keep your sessions to ten to twenty minutes. For the field protocol, you'll want to find a fenced-in area where you can work. The size of the area is not important; it could be a fenced-in backyard, baseball field, or tennis court. You'll also need a person or a dog or both to act as distractions. This training protocol works equally well if your dog is social with other dogs and just fine if they are not social because either way your dog will see the dog as a distraction. Allow your dog to run in the field or yard with their e-collar on while dragging their long leash. Walk with your dog as far away from the gate as you can. Have one of your friends approach the gate with a dog on a leash after you have been there for about five minutes practicing your recall, they will stay on the other side of the fence. When they approach the gate or fence you will tell your dog to go and say hello. Allow your dog to run over to the fence and do as they like. If your dog is not dog social it will be common for them to bark at the other dog and that is fine at the moment. If your dog wants to sniff the other dog through the fence or say hello to your friend that's fine too.

ALLOW the sniffing or barking for about five seconds and then say come and tap the T/V button. If your dog starts coming to you be sure to praise them as they come toward you and give them some praise and a treat when they reach you. If your dog stays at the fence and ignores the command, you'll give the command again and then hold down your continuous button and release it when they start coming toward you. If your dog is still not coming, repeat the come command and increase the level enough to get your dog to stop what they are doing and come toward you. If you lose control and are not able to salvage the recall, go to your longline to help your dog. Just a slight amount of pressure on the leash paired with the continuous e-collar stimulation will help them every time.

IF YOU FIND that your dog is struggling with these recalls, moving in closer to your dog can also help as your dog is likely struggling with the distance change. Practice this protocol a few times a day for the next three days until you have it mastered. The fence in this protocol serves four purposes.

- It keeps your dog from running away if you lose control
- It helps you, the owner, stay calm because nothing bad can happen
- It helps you, the owner, build confidence
- It adds not only safety to the protocol but frustration which

is something we want when starting to push our dogs in high distraction scenarios

WHEN YOUR DOG is able to recall away from dogs and people at the fence they are ready to go to the next step which is the transition protocol.

THE TRANSITION PROTOCOL is much like what you did in the last three days of training however now you are in the park with your dog or out for a hike and your dog is dragging the long leash. Take all the time you need with this step. Most dogs only need two to three days of dragging the leash before the owners feel comfortable taking the leash off completely.

YOUR DOG SHOULD BE COMING BACK NICELY but you may notice that your dog is running past you or running in your general direction and then wandering off. These are normal things to see at this stage in training and are easily fixed. You'll want to go back to the long leash for a few sessions so that you can step on the leash if needed when they run past you. When calling your dog back to you, if your dog comes toward you and starts to walk off, step on the long leash and hold the continuous button down on the e-collar, pick up the leash and help them back toward you. Release the button when they are right next to you. This little tweak will clean up the sloppiest of dogs because it creates some urgency for them to turn off the stimulation. When you have mastered this process, do the same but add a sit command ensuring that they feel the stimulation until they come to you and sit in front of you. You should now be able to take the long leash off and your dog should be much more responsive to coming directly to you instead of coming in your general area.

In this photo, you'll see one of my clients calling her dog away from myself and three dogs on the other side of the fence.

ANOTHER SIMPLE TWEAK that I like to do with clients is to take out the leash periodically during a walk or hike and attach it, and then take it off again right away. The reason we do this is to prevent dogs from avoiding the leash at the end of the walk. Some dogs will run away when they see the leash come out at the end of the walk, and this little tweak will help prevent your dog from thinking that when the leash comes out, we are going home.

CHECK out your (2) free step by step e-collar training video series at www.tedsbooks.com/watch

NEED HELP with your reactive dog? Check out my free 76 page e-book at https://www.tedsbooks.com/1-2/

PERIMETER TRAINING

*A*s with any other type of training, perimeter training must be done after the initial foundation training period has been completed. Many of my clients ask if we can do perimeter training if they have property that's not fenced. Let's begin with outlining some of the strengths and weaknesses of perimeter training when done with the e-collar and also with the use of a perimeter containment system.

PERIMETER TRAINING *with e-collar*
Strengths:

- No additional system needs to be purchased if you already have an e-collar
- The ability to be more subtle with the training if you're using an e-collar with 100 levels
- The ability to correct dirty thoughts if your dog is thinking about challenging the boundary
- The ability to quickly stop the stimulation if your dog challenges the boundary and is confused about how to turn off the stimulation

- The ability to perimeter train your dog on multiple properties easily

WEAKNESSES:

- You'll need to watch your dog more during the training period because you are the one responsible for turning on the stimulation if your dog tests the line

PERIMETER TRAINING **with a perimeter containment system**
Strengths:

- 100% consistency because the machine will turn the stimulation on and off for you
- The ability to utilize more of your property like the sides of your property that can be hard to self-monitor

WEAKNESSES:

- An additional unit is needed and must be installed
- Most perimeter containment systems don't have many levels of stimulation they can deliver. The average unit only has 3-6 levels, this makes subtle training much more challenging
- No ability to correct your dog for dirty thoughts if needed
- Difficult to move if your unit you have more than one property

To START perimeter training with your e-collar you will need to set up a visual boundary on your property to indicate where you want your dog to be free to enjoy and where you don't want them to go. A thin piece of rope or flags are commonly used for this purpose, I've even seen aerosol spray chalk used to indicate the boundary. Be strategic about how much property you perimeter train, more is not always better. If you have a front yard and a backyard, you can do both yards if you want, but I don't suggest the sides of your property because these are usually the areas that dogs will try and leave the yard if they gain the insight that they are not being watched constantly.

IT'S RECOMMENDED to perimeter train the yard that overlooks the area of your home that you spend the most time in. For example, my home has a yard in both front and back but we would only perimeter train the backyard because the kitchen and bedrooms where we spend the majority of our time when we are home are toward the rear of the house. You'll need to watch your dog during the training period and this is why it's not suggested to allow the boundary into the sides of the property.

WHEN USING A ROPE, position it at about the same height as your dog's eye level. Many of my clients will use a tree line by threading the rope throughout the trees. On properties without tree lines, you can drive some wooden stakes into the ground and thread the rope through the wooden stakes. **If utilizing the front yard be sure to leave at least 20-25 feet of buffer zone from the boundary to the road or sidewalk.** See the photo below for a suggested perimeter on this home.

IN THE PHOTO *above the white dotted line indicates a good boundary for this property because it's overlooking plenty of windows which will make it easier to watch your dog. Also notice how the side yard was not utilized because those areas tend to be the places where dogs will challenge the boundary when you are not looking.*

DAYS 1-3 of perimeter training

Your first step is to put your dog's e-collar on and attach a standard six to eight foot leash. Find the working level on the e-collar and begin by walking your dog up to the rope. As you walk past the line, most dogs will jump over the rope to continue walking with you. If that happens, hold down continuous button and walk your dog back onto into the perimeter and then release the button. You'll likely find that for the first few repetitions your dog will need help with the leash to go back into the perimeter. Continue ten to fifteen times. Don't say anything when your dog passes the line or goes back, this is critical. We want our dog to believe that the stimulation turned on because they passed the line. Again, don't verbally correct your dog for passing the line because if you do you'll likely have a dog later in training who challenges the line when you go inside the home if he thinks no one is watching him.

WHEN YOUR DOG understands the concept and will not go past the line even if you do, you can move to the next step in training. If you are not yet at this level and have been practicing for a few days, you may need to increase the e-collar level slightly and try again five to ten times. Before moving onto the next step, we should be able to walk across the line with your dog on a leash and have them stop at the line every time without any commands. Now you can take your dog to other areas of the yard and follow the same process. Switch to your long leash and allow your dog to drag it. If your dog follows you, hold down the continuous button, then release the button when he goes back behind the line. Always be willing to help with the leash if your dog has gotten confused. Do this five to ten times in all areas of the yard.

DAYS **4-7 of perimeter training**

At this stage, you can add distractions outside of the boundary. Start with lower distractions and work your way up to other dogs walking past your property. Start with a low e-collar working level and increase the level as needed depending on the distraction. It's still valuable to allow your dog to drag a long leash at this stage in training if you need to help them. It's important that during this entire process no commands are given when your dog is crossing the boundary. After about three weeks you can remove the visual boundary if you desire to. When your dog is doing a great job, take the long leash off and continue to add more distractions to ensure your dog's reliability. If you find that your dog is running up to the line and is thinking about running past the line when they see another dog across the street you can use the e-collar tone or continuous button to stop the progression of those dirty thoughts. Be sure to take your time because it's not an overnight process, but with some patience and training, you'll have a reliably trained dog who can enjoy your property in just a few weeks.

MANGO DOGS IS GROWING and we'll help you get up to speed on your dog training skills, handle all of your marketing and you'll be part of our team. For more information go to: www.mangodogs.com/join

THE IMPORTANCE OF USING AND
NOT USING COMMANDS

*a*t this stage in the training, you'll want to be sure to have your e-collar on your dog a lot more so that you can begin to stop any bad behaviors your dog has, such as excessive barking, jumping up on people, or pulling on the leash.

PREVIOUS CHAPTERS in this book have focused on properly communicating with your dog by teaching the concepts of the four pillars.

- Where the stimulation is coming from
- How to turn on the stimulation
- How to turn off the stimulation
- How to avoid the stimulation

AT THIS POINT, it may seem counterintuitive to suggest that you are now going to break away from the four pillars slightly but you'll have to trust me if you want to take your training to the next level.

· · ·

GOOD DOG TRAINING **works when the owner is present, great dog training works even if the owner is not present.**

LET'S unpack the commands and behaviors we will want to use a vocal command for. Commands like come, heel, sit, down, leave it, drop it, or go-to-bed are used to indicate something that you want your dog to do. Let's call these commands "action commands." These commands will always be given with a vocal command so that our dog understands the thing that we want them to do.

ON THE OTHER side of the spectrum, we have moments where we will not give commands like no, get down, stop jumping, and don't eat that. Let's call these behaviors "automatic avoidance behaviors." When dogs commit these deadly sins, I don't give any verbal cues, because they already know that when they feel a continuous stimulation that they can stop that stimulation by doing the exact opposite behavior. They already know that they can avoid stimulation by not doing specific behaviors.

When we use commands to stop these behaviors, some dogs will start to cheat when we are not around to watch. For example, if you tell your dog to not jump on people at the door, even if you use the e-collar to correct their behavior, it's likely that the moment your grandmother walks in the door two hours early for Christmas dinner, your dog is going to jump on her because you are in the bathroom taking a shower and your dog is waiting for you to say NO JUMPING.

USING commands when stopping bad behaviors does work, but trust me when I say it works better when you don't use commands because your dog associates their behavior with the correction. I don't want to have to constantly watch my dogs, I want them to not do these bad behaviors because they think that it's in their best interest regardless of whether I am present or not. More on this topic in the frequently asked questions section, see *jumping on people* and *dogs eating poop*.

THREE FORMS OF CORRECTION AND THE CONCEPT OF PUNISHMENT

E-COLLAR

Think of correction as a way for you to correct the course your dog is on when your dog is running across your front yard about to jump on someone or your dog is ignoring a command that you've given. Corrections can be verbal in nature, however, they tend to be most effective when they are paired with a physical reminder and the e-collar is a great way to usher in that reminder. Your e-collar level for corrections will commonly be at low/medium levels. However, there may be times where you need to increase the intensity drastically. Let's unpack the three types of correction and investigate the concept of punishment.

- Low-level suggestions
- Medium-level nudges
- High-level deterrents
- Punishment

HERE IS the simple method that I use to conclude what level intensity I should be working with. If the low-level stimulation is being ignored or your dog fixes their behavior and then quickly goes back to the unwanted behavior, you'll want to start to increase your level. When working at medium levels you should notice your dog avoiding the behaviors that you are indicating to them that you don't want them to do. If your dog is persistently committing unwanted behaviors you might need to jump up to the higher levels; these levels should not only change your dog's behavior in the short term but often they will also decrease the likelihood that your dog will misbehave in the future.

MANY TRAINERS like to promote the concept of low-level e-collar training, and I can sympathize with that terminology because it's easy to sell the concept to dog owners but that's not the entire story. Some dogs will need higher level corrections and if they are done to improve a dog's quality of life and keep that dog out of trouble, they are fine with me. The high levels are rarely used on most pet dogs and should never be used until other options have been given ample time to work first.

I THINK that the higher levels can be incredibly beneficial for some dogs because if your dog never discovers that the e-collar can deliver more than a slight tingle of stimulation, they may be more resistant and stubborn. A few weeks ago I had a husky mix in for training, he's a nice dog but very persistent, and if you know anything about huskies, they like to run away. We did three weeks of training with him which included thousands of repetitions of recall. Then we took him down to a lake with my dogs. The moment he saw the lake he went wild, running as fast as he could to the end of the long leash trying to get to the water. We stopped so that we could use the lake as a distraction as it was clear that he wanted nothing more than to run into the water and play. This dog's normal working level is around a 6-7/100 on the E-collar Technologies EZ900. We started him in the lower levels but when he clearly brushed that off we started training in the medium level territory, at this point the e-collar would stop him from lunging for about ten seconds and then he would start again. So I increased the level to high levels and he needed to go all the way up to 72/100. After just a few repetitions, he was really starting to get it. You could see a change in his behavior but also it was as though he learned that day that the e-collar can get rather uncomfortable if he continued to ignore what his owners wanted. A few days later, we met for another lesson and he was a completely different dog. Dash matured that day at the lake, and I'm excited to report that he's an off leash superstar now and the most reliable dog at the dog park. High-level corrections are useful for significantly decreasing the likelihood of reoffending with a behavior that you don't want.

PUNISHMENT IS RARELY USED in dog training because it's only good for extreme situations when nothing else has worked or when there are serious implications for your dog's health and safety if they do not listen to your commands. You'll most often see punishment used in situations like dogs running toward a busy road, chasing deer, getting into porcupines, and rattlesnake avoidance training. Punishment is designed to stop your dog in one stimulation from ever doing a specific behavior again. You don't get one failed repetition with rattlesnake avoidance training.

LAST SUMMER, two dogs died when hit by cars in the same week outside of a local dog park in my city. One dog was about to get into his owner's car and decided to bolt toward the road; sadly, that was his last run. The other dog chased a deer across that same road and was hit and killed instantly. These dogs were not e-collar trained, but in any case, if you find yourself with a 99% reliable dog, don't hesitate to safely set up training scenarios to make them safe because it could save your dog's life. A punishment is a high-level continuous e-collar stimulation in which the button is typically held down for several seconds.

· · ·

THE DIFFERENCE between a high-level correction and a punishment is the duration of the stimulation.

A HIGH-LEVEL CORRECTION is typically a quick press on a high level and a punishment is a high level for at least two to three seconds. It's imperative that high-level corrections and punishments are not used prematurely. It's very rare that I have to implement either of these techniques with the dogs that I train, so you should assume you never will with your dog.

LOW LEVELS HELP GUIDE, medium levels suggest, high levels decrease, and punishments stop behaviors forever.

DISTRACTIONS

WHAT YOUR DOG NEEDS TO KNOW

*R*eliability is paramount when we are training our dogs for obvious reasons. E-collar training can be an incredible way to develop the trust that only seeing can make you believe. Trust is developed each time you watch your dog make better choices. I'll never forget the first time I called my dog Phoenix back with the e-collar when he saw a red fox and started running after it. Saying that the feeling was incredible would be an understatement. I felt like I finally had control. Here is the uncomfortable truth about building that trust, it requires that you put your dog into positions where they will want to ignore your commands.

WHAT'S the perfect e-collar level when you are working around distractions? This is the million dollar question, and I'll answer it the way I've heard many other e-collar trainers explain the topic. There are only three e-collar levels, not enough, just right, and too high. Not enough, just right and too high are all subjective numbers on your e-collar because they entirely depend on the dog that you are working with. To make things even more complicated, not enough, just right, and too high change with each dog, but also change depending on the level of distractions you are working your dog around. If you get up in the middle of the night to go to the bathroom and you stub your toe, it hurts really badly. If you get up in the middle of the night because you hear someone breaking into your house and on your way to the back door you stub your toe, you won't feel the pain to the same degree. Your dog's pain threshold will change from inside to outside, from low distraction to high distraction, and you'll want to be ok with increasing your e-collar level once your dog has done all of the preliminary training outlined in the previous chapters.

RECENTLY, I had a former client call me about his two female dogs. He had done training with me a few years prior, and the dogs had done very well. His dogs were again completely out of control and he couldn't take it anymore. I told him to bring the dogs in as soon as possible and he did just that. When his dogs came out of the car, it was like an army was invading a new land. These dogs were even more out of control than they were before starting to train them. I couldn't get anywhere near them without them trying to bite me, so I told him to throw me the e-collar remote and we would go for a walk. He said that the dogs had been lunging and barking at every person and dog they saw, so he was apprehensive about going for a walk.

AS WE STARTED TO WALK, I noticed that the e-collar was set to 15/100 so I turned it all the way down to 1/100 and started to find the dogs' e-collar working levels. By the time I had reached 34/100 both dogs were walking nicely by his side, not pulling, not barking, perfect. They were completely changed, and I was able to pet them without any lunging or aggression. He turned around and looked at me with amazement as he asked, "what did you do?" I told him that I started at 1/100 and went up until I got to level 34/100. He stopped walking, and you could see that he seemed somewhat stunned. "34/100, really" he said. It was easy to spot his inability to understand what had just happened so I asked him if he had ever gone up to 34/100 before on the e-collar. He said no, and that he had never been past 22/100. When asking him why 22/100 he told me that 22/100 was the highest level I had gone up to in our private lessons that we had years ago. As you are training remember to watch out for that maximum level that you mentally develop.

THE MORAL OF this story is simple. After foundation training is done, use the level that you need to use. Some dogs are master manipulators and they will test you every way they can if they feel that you will not increase the level or if they see you hesitate to press the button.

CHECK out your (2) free step by step e-collar training video series at www.tedsbooks.com/watch

NEED HELP with your reactive dog? Check out my free 76 page e-book at https://www.tedsbooks.com/1-2/

FAQ PART 1

*efore utilizing the suggestions in this next section, please be
sure to have fully completed the requested foundation work.*

WHAT AGE DO *you start dogs with an e-collar?*

I have to start by saying that there is no right answer to this question. E-collar trainers typically use six months as a benchmark to denote when they start. Every trainer has a different thought on this, and no one trainer is right and no trainer is wrong. I rarely train dogs with an e-collar who are under the age of 8-9 months, but not because I think that less than 8 months is a bad idea. 8-9 months seems to be the age to which clients start to believe that what they are doing is not working. Most of these dogs start in puppy classes, then graduate to basic obedience only to continue to have issues. When these issues continue to get worse despite weekly training sessions and daily training from the dog owner, they seek a different solution and that's when they call me.

8-9 MONTHS of age is also an age in which many puppies will start to progress into adolescence and with this adolescence comes a newfound desire for freedom and an appetite to explore. While I see many dogs at 8-9 months, I see far more clients at 1.5-2.5 years. These clients follow the same trajectory in that, they start with puppy classes, then basic obedience, however many of them will then do another set of basic obedience classes hoping that the issues will resolve. When things don't get better, they wait another 12 months hoping that their dog will grow out of the issues before finally calling a better-rounded dog trainer.

Knowing the best time to start is more of an art than a science. I don't suggest under the age of 6 months solely for the reason that people at the park often throw a fit if they notice a young puppy wearing an e-collar, and I want to spare the client that drama. The truth is that when e-collar training is done correctly with the right tool, it can be done more gently than many other forms of more socially acceptable things that puppy owners do. Often I see puppy owners allowing their puppies to pull them into pet shops, all the while they are hacking and coughing because their collar is physically hurting their trachea, yet pet store owners never suggest that the dog owner is doing anything abusive. Try taking a puppy into a pet shop with an e-collar on. Even if the puppy is acting like a perfect gentleman, people will treat the dog owner like they are Hitler himself. The owners of the pulling puppy are lovingly up-sold on a new harness, but the e-collar trained puppy owner is ostracized.

How do I transition off of the e-collar?

The vast majority of dog owners will transition off the e-collar too soon which can be detrimental to your goal of having a reliable dog. I've seen clients get to a place where they thought they were ready to transition off the e-collar who would then stop having their dog wear the e-collar. These clients would have reliable dogs when wearing the e-collar but they would make the mistake of putting the e-collar in the closet when progressing off the e-collar. The cold turkey method may work if you're quitting smoking but is a terrible idea in e-collar training; instead, we'll use the 10+15 day method outlined below.

If your dog is not wearing the e-collar, you can't guarantee reliability and compliance with your commands. You'll be tempted to wean off of the e-collar before your dog is ready, but you'll need to be 100% consistent with your training for at least six weeks before thinking about transitioning off the e-collar. After six weeks have passed and you think your dog is ready, you will continue to allow them to wear the e-collar for the transitioning period. For the next ten days, you'll be only giving the T/V with your commands. If your dog is able to go ten days wearing the e-collar and you've not needed to follow those T/V commands with a correction, you can progress to the next fifteen days. If during the ten-day period you need to follow up your T/V commands with corrections you are not ready to transition off the e-collar.

If all went perfectly in the first ten days, you can progress to the next fifteen days. In this stage, you'll continue to have your dog wear the e-collar and eliminate the T/V commands. If your dog can do fifteen days without the need of T/V of correction when given commands, you are ready to leave your e-collar unit in the closet. If your dog needs T/V or correction in this stage, you'll need to go back to using the e-collar for some time until your dog is able to pass the 10+15 day method test.

How do I use an e-collar if my dog has already worn a bark collar or perimeter fence collar before?

Dogs with previous bark collar or perimeter collar use will require additional steps in the training process that should be done before you start your e-collar training. Some dogs who have had previous bark collar or perimeter training will be apprehensive about e-collar training because of their previous experience with a collar that looks like this new tool you are putting on their neck. Remember that there is nothing inherently positive about bark collars, so most dogs hate them. With perimeter training, the dogs are less likely to shy away from the collar itself because most of these dogs associate the freedom of going outside with the collar.

LET'S unpack a few things you can do to make the e-collar process a positive one for these dogs. Always put a leash on your dog before putting the e-collar on and always give your dog a treat and some praise when putting on the e-collar. When you start your e-collar training, you will take an extra week of training before starting the above outlined foundation period. This additional week is designed to convince your dog that the e-collar is not a bad thing. Because of your dog's previous bark collar or perimeter training, they will be expecting the low-level e-collar stimulation to quickly get more uncomfortable because they have that association from the previous tools. This is why we do this additional step. This step cannot be done with an e-collar with less than 100 levels because if you have an e-collar with only 10 levels, each additional level will prove to be too large of a jump in stimulation. The key here is to use an incredibly subtle level that your dog will hardly show you that they feel it. I often tell clients doing this training that if they think they might be able to see their dog noticing the e-collar, that's the right level.

TO BEGIN this additional step you can start by finding the most subtle e-collar working level on your dog; when you've found that level say your dog's name and then tap the continuous stimulation once. Directly after this, you'll give your dog his favorite treat and give him some praise. It's suggested to do this process outside when you are on walks. You can continue on your walk and do this about five to ten times on your walk. Practice this twice a day for seven days, then start your e-collar foundation training as described in Chapter 2.

. . .

40

Training small dogs

Training a small dog is no different than training a medium, large or extra large-sized dog. The concepts are entirely the same. For many years training small dogs with an e-collar was not an option. The e-collars were far too large and heavy for small dogs, but more importantly, they were unable to get a consistent connection on the dog's neck because they were not designed for small dogs. Small dog owners today have a lot more options! In general, the collars are much smaller and lighter, but we now have one e-collar that is specifically designed for extra small/small dogs. The Micro from E-Collar Technologies is hands down the best e-collar on the market for smalls dogs. I say it's the best because it's lightweight, compact and the contact points are closer together, which is essential when training a small dog.

Two small dog owners have e-mailed me in the last 24 hours asking for guidance. One purchased the ET300 Mini from E-collar Technologies and the other owner had purchased the EZ900. Both of those e-collars are incredible units but they are not made specifically for small dogs. It was for that reason that I suggested they buy comfort pads from www.ecollar.com.

A comfort pad will help to distribute the e-collar stimulation over 4-6 contact points. This will prevent any possible irritation and most importantly, it will decrease the distance between the contact points. You can even order comfort pads for the Micro e-collar if you are concerned about the same issue. Small dogs have small necks and this is why it's so critical to have an e-collar like the Micro, or use a small-medium dog e-collar like the Mini or EZ900 with a comfort pad. All of the different comfort pad combinations can be purchased at www.ecollar.com

STEALING *food from the counter*

I know you love your dog, but that pork chop should stay on your counter. It's vital to remember that when tackling this issue, you'll not be giving any commands as we want our dog to avoid stealing food both when you are present and when you are absent.

1. PUT your dog in a room like a bathroom for two minutes while you setup the protocol. We don't want our dog to see what we are about to do.

2. Put your dog's e-collar on, and be sure that it's turned on.

3. Place a small-medium sized spoon on the edge of your counter and bait it with something delicious. It's best to use an aromatic bait like peanut butter or a piece of hot dog.

4. Select the correct e-collar level, by setting your e-collar level to whatever your general working level is inside the home and adding ten levels. For example, if my dog's e-collar working level in the home was 13/100, the level for this protocol would start at 23/100. If you have a dog who's extremely sensitive to the e-collar stimulation, then feel free to determine the appropriate level for your dog.

5. Let your dog out of the bathroom, take the remote with you when you go into another room, and do something like watch a movie or work on your laptop.

6. When you hear the spoon hit the ground, you'll hold the continuous button for about 1 second and not say anything.

7. After the first correction, wait fifteen to thirty minutes to go get the spoon and add some more bait. Increase your level by 10 every time you have to set up the protocol again.

NO COMMANDS ARE NEEDED HERE because it could create a dog that still steals food when you have left the home. Your dog already knows that stealing food is something you loathe, so now you're simply following through with your ability to correct your dog when they think you can't. Why would we start at a level that is ten levels above the normal working level? Because this is one of the very few situations where your dog will actually be given the opportunity to get something they want. A gentle correction at the working level will not deter dogs from stealing food as the level of positive motivation the food offers is higher than the subtle negative motivation from the e-collar. You should see rapid results by using this protocol. It's normal for clients to be able to stop counter surfing for the rest of their dog's life in just one day of training.

IT MUST BE NOTED that if you have more than one dog, you'll want to add a camera so that you can determine which dog should be corrected. You'll need a camera on the counter and a monitor that you can take with you to another area of your home or apartment. Often my clients will use a tablet and a smartphone linked with skype or facetime. If you use a camera be sure to put your camera on mute so that you don't tip off the dog that you're watching.

. . .

DOGS EATING *poop*

Please be sure to consult with your Veterinarian to check for things like diabetes, cushings, thyroid issues, incomplete diets, and parasites. If your Veterinarian has eliminated any potential medical reasons for the feces eating and you have done your e-collar foundation training, you can now move on to stopping this detestable behavior.

IN 2010, a female labrador retriever named Dax came into our lives. At the time she loved to eat feces. Rabbit, horse, cow, dog, cat, you name the animal and she was game. She was incredible at sniffing the stuff out, and much to my discontent with her behavior she was really talented at it. On many off leash hikes, she could be found digging up prehistoric tyrannosaurus poop from 73 million years ago. She wasn't picky. After her e-collar foundation training was done we got straight to work on her taboo love affair. I'm happy to announce that she's not eaten a piece in eight years thanks to e-collar training.

AFTER COMPLETING your e-collar foundation training, you can get started. This training protocol does not require any treats or praise or even a command to not eat feces because it's an implied behavior. Don't eat poop... ever. Start with your dog on a long leash. Take your dog out to an area where you know your dog will find feces. Start at ten levels above your regular e-collar working level. When your dog smells some feces and starts to hone in on the scent and is about one foot from the feces hold down the continuous button on the e-collar. Allow 2 seconds, and If your dog is undeterred, you can increase the level. I much prefer a quality e-collar here like models by E-collar Technologies because they have the versatility to hold down the continuous button and increase the level all at the same time. As you continue to hold down the button, increase the level rather quickly until your dog stops. Do not use a command here like "no eating poop" because we want our dog to assume the action of eating poop or even sniffing feces is the mechanism that turns on the stimulation. If your e-collar is not able to increase the level without releasing the continuous button, release the button and increase the level by 10 and re-apply. When your dog walks away from the feces, act like nothing has happened as you keep walking down the street or trail. Typically I will turn down the level of the e-collar slightly before approaching the next pile of distraction because I want my dog to see that the e-collar stimulation gets more intense the closer they get to the poop.

WHEN YOU'RE SEEING your dog start to avoid the feces, you can allow them off leash as you continue to watch them. I usually allow for three to four corrections on the leash before progressing off leash. If your dog is still trying to take advantage of opportunities, you can progress by starting at a higher level. It should be noted that after just a few days of this training, I don't like to allow dogs to smell the feces even if they don't eat it because this often leads to them starting to eat again in the future.

JUMPING *up on people*

This is one of the most common behavioral issues that I help my clients with. The e-collar is an exceptional tool to use for this issue because it's a tool that can be used at a distance and because it's a non-emotional tool. If your dog eats poop and we use the e-collar, it doesn't matter if your dog likes poop after the training, in fact, we don't want your dog to like poop if they are a feces eater. Stopping a dog from jumping up, however, is solved in a similar fashion, but the training is much more nuanced because we do want our dog to continue to be social with people when the training is done. You'll want to take extra time during this process and remember that we will also be reinforcing your dog for not jumping with treats and praise.

. . .

INSIDE THE HOME or outside off leash, the training protocol is the same. Start by setting your level to the working level and add just a few additional levels. For example, if your dog's e-collar working level is typically 12/100 inside the house, set your e-collar to 14-15/100. Allow a friend or family member to come into the home and instruct them to ignore your dog for the first few repetitions. If your dog jumps on them, you'll hold down the continuous button when they jump and release it when they stop jumping. Neither you or the person coming into your home should give a command when this is happening as it's an implied behavior, and we want our dog to think that the stimulation is coming from the act of jumping, not from the person entering the door.

SOME DOGS ARE QUICK JUMPERS. They jump up without notice, and before you can say son-of-a-gun, they've stopped jumping. With this type of jumper, you'll need to have your finger on the continuous button ready to press for a quick jump. These dogs will typically need you to increase the level a little more because a quick tap at a low level is often not enough to stop them from jumping. For the dogs that jump and stay up, the process is done in much the same way, nonetheless, you'll need to hold the button down for longer, and I typically suggest a lower level for these sustained jumps and hugs. In either case, if you find that your dog is ignoring these lower levels, you can increase the level as needed, but be sure to remember that if you increase the level too much this can cause your dog to not want to approach people, so be sure to take your time.

WHEN YOUR DOG is excelling at the training, you can instruct your friends and family to be more animated with your dog, at the same time you can put a bowl of treats outside your door for friends to have access to some tasty tidbits for the times they enter and your dog does not jump on them. If they don't jump, your friend or family member can pull out a treat and throw it on the floor for them as they tell them, good boy or good girl. People should not have to train your dog when they come to your home. You'll be doing that part, they should not have to completely avoid your dog and ignore them when they come to your home. When people come to my home, they can get my dogs as excited as they want and my dogs will not jump.

PULLING on the leash

Pulling on the leash is an issue the majority of my clients' dogs have when we start training. Often, we will see this issue disappear in the first few weeks because my clients are working on their homework while going out for walks. If you've done the foundation work and are still struggling with this issue you can try a few more techniques. The technique I use the most for these persistent pullers is the stop and pop method. In this method you will take your dog for a walk with a six to eight foot leash; it's good to give them a little more room while working on this technique. At the moment just before your dog starts to pull, you'll stop quickly and tap the continuous button at the same time. I always set the level at least 10 levels higher than the working level. If your dog persists you can increase the level some more until you have a dog who is walking with slack on the leash. Another technique I use is the pressure/release technique. In this technique, you will add low/medium level continuous pressure every time your dog starts to pull and release the button when they stop pulling. Always start your sessions at a low level and increase as needed. I have a book focusing on this very issue called *Prong Collar Training for Pet Dogs*. If you are interested in that book, on my website at www.tedsbooks.com.

HOW FAR SHOULD my dog range away from me?

You should find that your dog does not range too far away from you at this point in your training, most dogs keep within fifty to one hundred feet. In general, I don't allow dogs to be out of sight because they could find a porcupine or a similar animal without you knowing until it's too late.

. . .

MANGO DOGS IS GROWING and we'll help you get up to speed on your dog training skills, handle all of your marketing and you'll be part of our team. For more information go to: www.mangodogs.com/join

FAQ PART 2

an the e-collar cause burns, or other medical issues for my dog?
Since the inception of e-collars in the late 1950s, there
have always been rumors circulating about the safety of e-collars. The
best way for me to dispel such myths is to try and influence your
opinion on what the stimulation coming from an e-collar feels like.
They feel like the stimulation that is produced from a TENS unit, a
commonly used machine in chiropractic and physiotherapy clinics.
This stimulation feels more like a pulse. At lower levels, people often
report that it feels like it's tickling them. At low levels, the stimulation
produced by a quality e-collar is hardly an offensive feeling. At higher
levels, the stimulation gradually stops feeling like a little twitch or
tickle in the finger and starts to feel more intense and it can be very
uncomfortable at high levels to humans and dogs but it's not harmful
in any way. I can speak from personal experience because I've had
many different e-collars on my neck at the maximum level and I've
never had my neck burned or altered in any way.

Can my dog swim with their e-collar on?

Check your e-collar to ensure that it's capable to be used while
your dog is swimming. All quality brands will have full waterproofing

50

but some of the lesser quality brands produce e-collars with inferior quality, and these e-collars are not to be trusted around water. Generally speaking, if you don't buy an e-collar from trusted manufacturers like E-Collar Technologies, Dogtra, or Sportdog, I would not trust the e-collar in the water. E-collar stimulation does not become more powerful when introduced to water. Roughly 15% of the stimulation will actually dissipate into the water, this is why I tell my clients to increase their e-collar level by 2-5 levels out of 100 when their dog is swimming.

How often should *your dog wear the e-collar?*

When you start training your dog with an e-collar, you will want to have your e-collar on your dog only during your two lessons each day. This method is met with some disdain from other e-collar trainers, but there is a method to the madness. Most e-collar trainers would have clients believe that their dog should be wearing the e-collar essentially 16-18 hours a day, only taking it off at night for sleeping time. I don't subscribe to this way of thinking for two reasons;

1. THE FIRST few weeks of training will be spent doing e-collar conditioning, and thus the e-collar will only be needed for 2-3 quick sessions each day

2. If the e-collar is placed on the dog for 18 hours each day and is not used to correct bad behavior during the conditioning phase, it's my opinion that this fact aids many dogs in becoming collar smart

RATHER THAN SUGGESTING that my clients use the e-collar all day, I tell them to have the e-collar on their dog for the two quick lessons each day when their dog will be trained with the e-collar. After the conditioning phase has been completed, they should have the e-collar on their dog when they are doing things with their dog that will require assistance with the e-collar.

. . .

AFTER THE CONDITIONING PHASE, you'll need to determine which one of the following categories your dog falls into.

GOOD IN THE HOME, *naughty outside the home;*
If your dog is perfect in the home but struggles to focus when outside of the home, you are not alone.

GOOD OUTSIDE, *naughty inside the home;*
A more rare combination to be seen, some dogs are fabulous outside of the home but exhibit the majority of their issues inside the home.

NAUGHTY *in the home and naughty outside the home;*
Most of the dogs that I work with fit into this category. They struggle both indoors and outdoors.

HOW MUCH YOU use your e-collar will be directly linked to where your dog struggles to pay attention. Most of my clients' dogs will use the e-collar only for 2-3 lessons daily until conditioning is complete, then use the e-collar in large part when they go outside to help with recall, pulling on the leash and other behavioral issues.

IF YOUR DOG also needs help with issues that are happening inside of the home, you'll want to have your e-collar on your dog when scenarios present themselves that might require the e-collar. Your dogs should never sleep with their e-collars on, and as mentioned numerous times in this book, be sure to rotate your e-collar on your dog's neck if the e-collar is on for more than 2-4 hours. To that point, don't leave your dog's e-collar on them if you leave the home to go to work.

PREVENTING IRRITATION FROM THE E-COLLAR?

One thing that I dislike about e-collars is that they can cause irritation on a dog's neck if they are left on for too long, or if your dog has skin sensitivities that need to be addressed. Luckily, these irritation issues are extremely rare and can be easily remedied if they do pop up. The most common type of irritation is a simple redness that can be noticed on some dogs' skins where the e-collar was resting, this is rather common, but hardly ever noticed because most dogs have enough fur to camouflage the redness. This redness does not need to be addressed, but it can be helped by transitioning to different contact points on your e-collar. I prefer contact points that are made out of titanium or copper for such irritation. Try the hypoallergenic titanium contact points or comfort pads from E-Collar Technologies they are available at www.ecollar.com. Contact points from www.ecollar.com will fit most other e-collar brands, but it's essential that you check your e-collar to be sure before placing your order.

IF YOU ARE NOTICING A MORE serious irritation that seems to have produced an infection, this can be caused by several things. Most often it's seen when clients are leaving their e-collar on for a very long time without rotating it or taking it off. The medical term for this is called pressure necrosis. I've only seen this 3 times in my entire career, so it's not very common.

ANOTHER CAUSE for infection can be seen when dogs are wearing the e-collar in bacterial dense scenarios. This scenario is also extremely rare, but I've seen a few dogs that spend a lot of time in rivers and lakes in the hot summer months that have had an infection in the area where they were wearing the e-collar. This is easily preventable and relatively easy to treat if your dogs find themselves with such a sore. If your dog is swimming with their e-collar on, be sure to wash it with warm soapy water once daily to help disinfect it from bacteria. You should also be sure to take off the e-collar after swimming and allow your dog some time to rest in an area where their neck will quickly dry before putting the e-collar back on, a fan is great to help with this. Moist fur and a bacterial infested e-collar are not a great combination.

IF YOUR DOG has a mild red skin irritation, Vet assistance is not required. Changing your contact points should solve that issue. If your dog has an infection, you will notice a discharge that will be sticking to your dog's fur. This infection can spread rapidly and is referred to as a hot spot. It's important to note that plenty of dogs that don't wear e-collars at all, get hot spots and they seem to be most commonly seen on Golden Retrievers. You should take your dog to the Vet for this type of issue. One of my dogs had one of these hot spots recently on his back and the Vet shaved fur from the area and gave me a cream to put on it. The infection was gone in a few days.

WHAT SHOULD *I do if I make a mistake with the e-collar?*

Welcome to the real world. You will make mistakes, but as I like to remind myself, mistakes are just reminders from God, showing me what not to do the next time. If you hit the button by accident, don't make a big scene, and your dog will get over it quickly. Have you ever stepped on your dog's foot by accident when out for a walk with your dog? We all have, right? Did you stop walking your dog? No, you told your dog that you were sorry and you kept walking. Your dog doesn't hate you, does he? Do they no longer want to go for walks? Move past the incident, think about what you did incorrectly, and do your best not to replicate the issue in the future.

Do you use e-collars to teach new behaviors?

Overwhelmingly, e-collar trainers teach new behaviors using

methods that are the same as those methods that a positive reinforcement trainer would use. If you are not familiar with the world of dog training, these methods are typically referred to as shaping. Shaping is simply the act of encouraging the dog to do the desired behavior using something that they desire, and in most cases, that desire is a food reward. Using the food to move the dog's nose, and in turn, move the dog's body is really all that shaping is. Teaching a dog commands like, sit, down, or come is really rather simple. We start with the dog on a leash, in a low distraction environment. We put food in our hands and slowly move the hand in the direction that we want the dog's body to move. In the context of teaching a dog to sit, we put the food in front of the dog's nose, and slowly move it towards us, when the dog moves just a few inches, we slowly move the hand upward and then back just 3-6 inches. If the dog is paying attention they will follow the lure into a sitting position. Then, we tell the dog a cue to let them know that what they have done is correct, and finally, we give them the food reward. We do this for about 10-15 minutes and then, end the first session. We come back and do another session later that same day to solidify the position. Notice that we are not using any commands yet, introducing commands at this stage will only serve to confuse the dog. After 2-3 days in which we do 2-3 sessions like this, we then add the word that we want the dog to recognize, in this case, sit.

IF YOU ARE READING this book, chances are that you own a dog that struggles to do what you ask them to do in the face of distraction. Essentially 100% of my clients come in and ask for help after already seeking a positive training council. They are frustrated because their dog already understands what they are being asked to do, yet will not do it at times. They know what come means, but do not come when the distraction is larger than the positive reward that they will receive when they return to their owner.

E-COLLAR TRAINERS ARE SIMPLY trainers who are willing to set proper boundaries when their students already know a command and do not perform the command, or when they choose to exhibit an egregiously out of control behavior. When a positive reinforcement trainer is struggling to break through to a dog, they have an internal struggle brewing and the answers don't ever serve the dog owner. The positive trainer may tell their clients that their dogs are "over threshold" which simply means that their dogs are too distracted, or they will instruct the dog owner to become more interesting. The client needs to get better treats and use more enthusiasm, and still, in many cases, these dogs will not respond, so they are then told that they should stop walking their dog entirely. Pardon my massive overgeneralization of positive trainers, but it's just what I see locally in my area. Because these dog owners do not desire to live a sheltered life with their dog, the client transitions to a balanced trainer who is willing to keep the dog accountable.

So, we e-collar trainers don't use correction to teach behaviors, but we do use it to reinforce behaviors that they already know, and we do use it to stop bad behaviors that the dog knows we do not like. Your dog knows that you hate it when they pull on the leash or bark aggressively at other dogs. The key is to show them that those behaviors will not be tolerated, and then to give them the things that they desire (food, toys, praise) when they make a better decision.

FAQ PART 3

redatory animal chasing technique?
As you'll remember from the opening story in this book, my dog Phoenix was a killing machine. He lived to kill animals, and if you have a dog like Phoenix, you'll want to pay attention to how I fixed his issues. Any dog trainer who is reading this likely just spat up what they were drinking because we dog trainers hate to imply that you can fix anything as intense as predatory chasing. The thing is, you can if you know what you are doing and are using the right tool.

BEFORE I TELL you how to address the issue, I need to outline when this protocol should be used and when it should not be used. This protocol is for intense dogs that can kill animals or dogs, not for fun-loving dogs that chase squirrels in the park for excitement, a simple recall will aid you for that.

BACK IN THE DAY, I was told to use a technique called a crittering protocol. This protocol was done with an e-collar, and so I thought that it would be effective. Not true. I was instructed to take my dog to a field, with a cat placed inside of a dog crate as a distraction. With my dog at a large distance away, I was to allow him to smell the cat just for a moment and then use the lowest level possible on the e-collar to get my dog to turn away from the cat, at which point I was supposed to praise him for looking away from the cat. Needless to say, this protocol worked great, until the cat moved, or until we found ourselves in a situation involving a cat that I wasn't expecting. When we were at the park and a rabbit would run across the trail, my dog would run with all of his momentum towards the rabbit, despite my attempt at playing tickle me Elmo's e-collar training.

THE PROTOCOL that I have called the Don't Chase Animals protocol is very similar to the crittering protocol mentioned above, however, it actually works if dogs are desiring to kill animals, and it works in moments that you are not expecting. It's also important to remind readers that you must have finished all of the e-collar conditioning homework before starting this protocol. Start with your dog on a long leash, 25 feet is ideal. I like to put the dog in a harness so that if they hit the end of the leash with a lot of force, they will not hurt themselves. With your dog wearing the harness and long leash, take your dog to a place that you know will contain things that your dog will want to chase and hunt. Parks with wildlife are ideal training areas for this, remember that you should be holding on to the end of the leash with a firm grip. When your dog sees one of these animals, allow them to get overstimulated, don't try to calm them down. When they run to the end of the leash, hold the continuous button on your e-collar for 3 seconds at its highest level and then release. Your dog will likely vocalize at that moment, but that is ok. Remember that what you are doing could save their life, and it will not have to be done many times to prove effective. Then call your dog back to you, and keep walking, act as nothing happened. Go about the rest of your walk and see if you need to reapply again, most dogs don't hit the end of the leash again. Do the same thing for two more walks, one day apart from each other. When you can go three days without having your dog hit the end of the leash, you can move on to the next stage. Now it's time to let them drag the long leash. If they run more than 25 feet from you, step on the leash and reapply the correction for 4 seconds at the highest level. When you can do 3 walks with the leash dragging and no running at animals, then proceed to the final step, off-leash. Do the same as before without the leash.

If desired, you can use a command here directly before the correction like Leave It, I do this because I allow my dogs the freedom to run after squirrels, but not other animals like rabbits, skunk, and porcupine.

The reason I say that these types of issues can be fixed is that my dog Phoenix was able to live with three cats in harmony after this protocol, with or without the e-collar. The proof is in the pudding as they say. Only use this protocol if you have tried others that have not worked and your dog is a killing machine that needs reform.

Can the e-collar be used with aggressive dogs?

For many years, the majority of e-collar manufacturers have stated in their owner's manuals that e-collars should not be used on aggressive dogs. This is clearly a decision that has been pushed by their legal council in an effort to mitigate legal responsibility. I know hundreds of e-collar trainers around the world, and all but a hand full of them use the e-collar in some form or another when working with reactive or aggressive dogs. Aggression has been my specialty for over a decade, and I've rehabilitated thousands of dogs over the years. I can confidently say that e-collars are a game-changer for aggressive dogs when they are used with the right technique.

This topic is a massive one, which is why wanted to share a free e-book with you on the topic. All that you have to do is go to https://

www.tedsbooks.com/1-2/ Download Stopping Leash Reactivity today.

***WHAT IS** the difference between a momentary stimulation, continuous stimulation, vibration, and tone?*

Any quality e-collar will have a variety of modes that you can use to train your dog. The most commonly used modes would be momentary, continuous, vibration and tone. Momentary stimulation is also known as Nick on Dogtra e-collars, and you can think of it as a quick poke. If you want to feel what this stimulation feels like, take your e-collar, turn the level to 1 and tap the momentary button, increase the level until you feel the sensation. If you hold the button down, the stimulation will not stay on, which is why they call it momentary stimulation. Many trainers use this mode exclusively, but it's not a mode that I use often.

IF YOU DESIRE A QUICK CORRECTION, it makes much more sense to use continuous stimulation mode. With this mode, you can tap the button, or hold it down, and the dog will feel the sensation until you release the button. This mode makes much more sense as it's like having the best of both worlds, a quick tap if you need it, or a longer stimulation if that's what your training requires. The continuous mode is by far the button that I will use most on my e-collar when training with clients because it's the most versatile.

THE VIBRATION MODE feels exactly how you would expect it to feel, like a cell phone vibrating in your pocket. I uncommon that I use this mode because I find that about 20% of dogs are visibly uncomfortable with the sensation of the vibration, I've seen dogs bolt away from the owner when they feel the vibration. I do however use it to help with recall if I'm training a dog that has been trained on an invisible fence unit. With perimeter fences, the collar will beep to warn the dog to stay away from the invisible line that they are not supposed to cross.

With these dogs, I like to stay away from using the tone, as they often have a negative association with the tone, and this is why I prefer to use the vibration in such a case.

THE TONE IS a mode that I was always told to stay away from, and still to this day few e-collar trainers use it. I use it in some ways like a clicker. You did something good, so come and get a reward. The important part is that if your dog is wearing the e-collar, they will always hear the tone because the sound comes right from the collar which is just inches from their ear. The beauty of the tone is that it can be followed with a momentary or continuous stimulation if the dog refuses to come to the owner. Let's be honest, e-collars are not as effective as they are because they are more advanced tools of communication. Surely they are helpful in that way, but they are effective because they give the dog owner the ability to physically address an issue even if their dog is 500 feet away from them. Tone or vibration is nothing without the ability to create a sense of urgency, and that's where the momentary or continuous thrive. In my style of e-collar training, I only use the Tone and Continuous modes.

VIBRATION ONLY COLLARS

Some dog owners desire to train their dogs without any type of uncomfortable feeling, and this is the niche that vibration-only collars are attempting to fill. I've always been extremely skeptical of electric collars that only vibrate because I know dog behavior well enough to know that the only real situation these collars could be useful would be for training deaf dogs.

IN FULL TRANSPARENCY, I have little knowledge of these collars. I've seen a few friends use them from time to time to train extremely easy-going dogs, with overly sensitive clients. A few years ago, I had a young man come in for training with his Akita puppy of 10 months of age. She was starting to growl excessively at other dogs and people pulled excessively on the leash and had a terrible recall when off-leash. He came in to chat about training options and pricing when I suggested e-collar training to help. The next day he called me to thank me for meeting with him and mentioned that he wanted to sign up for the program that I suggested. "Just one catch" he mentioned. "My girlfriend doesn't want to use an e-collar, but I convinced her to let us use a vibration collar instead". Despite my better judgment, I told him that I would order him a vibration collar and that it would not work well for his dog. "You'll be wasting your money, and you will end up buying an e-collar anyways," I told him. He insisted that he needed to keep his girlfriend happy and that this was the best way to do it.

WE START their training a week later and all was going well for the first week but his dog started ignoring the vibration collar in the second week. She was overweight and not even taking treats when offered, so I asked the client to cut her food back a little which would get some food desire built. "She'd kill me if I did that," he said. "Listen, man, I know that you love this girl and everything, but it's your dog, not hers. How am I supposed to help you and your dog if I can't use anything negative, and your dog is not even motivated by anything positive?" He indicated that he would talk to his girlfriend that night in an effort to find a suitable solution for everyone. Two days later he emailed me saying that his dog had acted terribly at the park the day before and that he wanted to stop training. He was not being given the freedom to build a food drive, and his dog was ignoring the vibration collar, so he figured that he had no further options. It's extremely rare that a client will quit one of my programs, so the situation taught me a valuable lesson.

TWO MONTHS LATER, the client called me to ask me if I could order him an e-collar. I asked about his girlfriend and she was out of the picture. With that, we built his dog's food drive over the next few weeks and started e-collar training, and the client couldn't be happier with the results. Certainly, not all dogs need an e-collar to behave well, but when a dog starts to develop issues, especially off-leash issues, the dog will learn to avoid commands, and they too will learn to avoid vibration collars. Traditional e-collar training is far more effective because the level of discomfort can be so low that the dogs can hardly feel it, yet the e-collar also has the ability to become more intense if needed. It's this small discrepancy that makes all the difference.

raining a deaf dog with an e-collar
Training a deaf dog can be done in many ways. Hand signals, vibration collars, e-collars, the options are abundant. Some trainers only train with hand signals which in my estimation is a big mistake. If a deaf dog is running away from you, they can't see your hand signals, which is why it's crucial to have a tool like a vibration collar or e-collar.

WHILE MANY DOG owners want to select a vibration collar to use as a communication delivery system, I believe that e-collars are a much better investment because of their versatility. When training a deaf dog, you can't use vocal commands of any kind and so you need to use a combination of hand signals and physical cues to let the dog know what you expect of them. The best deaf dog training is done with a mixture of hand signals for basic commands like sit, down, come, heel, and the e-collar will guide the dog when they are distracted. You start by training your dog in a low distraction environment to understand specific cues given with your hands. Teaching those hand cues is beyond the scope of this book, so you can find videos on YouTube that will show you how. Once your dog is fluent in these hand gestures, you can move outside with your dog on a long leash and e-collar. This step will help your dog pay attention when outside.

THE E-COLLAR VIBRATION will be used when you are attempting to get your dog's attention. To do this you'll allow your dog to look away from you, then hold the vibration button down until they turn around and look at you, then give them a cue to tell them that they made a good choice, (many deaf dog owners give a thumbs up) then give your dog a treat or some food. Practice this by walking in your yard, or a local park with your dog attached to you by a 15-foot long leash. Practice twice daily for 10 minutes per session. Personally, I suggest that this is the only way these dogs should eat. This way, the vibration becomes like a cue to come and get food, and it's hard to resist if the food is only delivered when outside doing recall training.

AFTER ABOUT A WEEK OF TRAINING, your dog should be capable of looking away from you, then looking to you when they feel the vibration. I much prefer to teach the vibration outside, as teaching inside can cause more sensitive dogs to be fearful of it. Now you will blend your e-collar's continuous stimulation into the training. Again outside with your long leash and e-collar on your dog, take your dog to a slightly more distracting area. Allow your dog to look away from you, hold the vibration button for 1-2 seconds. If they come running to you, feed them and praise them. If they are too distracted, you can start using your continuous stimulation mode. Start at level one, tap the button 2-3 times. Then go up to level 2, tap 2-3 times. Continue until you see your dog respond to the stimulation. You will already be confident in finding the e-collar working level from the previous 3 weeks of e-collar foundation training. The reaction should be very subtle. When you find that level, keep holding that continuous button until they turn around and look in your direction, then release the button. When your dog comes to you and is looking at you, you can give them a thumbs up and some food or their favorite treat.

. . .

THE NEXT SECTION of training focuses on much of the same, but you will allow your dog to drag the long leash while you are practicing. Practice twice daily until your dog is responding well, then take the leash off completely in a large fenced-in area. Finally, finish your training in an off-leash area without a leash to ensure that your dog is reliable.

THIS TRAINING IS BROKEN up into four major sections;

1. TRAIN your dog to understand hand signals

2. Train your dog to understand that they should turn around and look at you when they feel the e-collar vibrate

3. Train your dog to understand that they can't ignore you when they are off-leash, this is done with the continuous stimulation mode

4. Train with and without a long leash in off-leash contexts to ensure recall reliability

CAN I use an e-collar on my fearful dog?

It's often said that fearful dogs should never be trained with any level of force, and while I agree with these sentiments in large part, I also disagree with them in certain contexts. It's my view that very few dogs are truly fearful, so we must start with definitions. A fearful dog is a dog who avoids conflict. They shy away from things that make them uncomfortable. So, if you own a dog that shies away from things, your dog will be well served to stay away from methods that use negative motivations. When a dog is scared of new people, or dogs, and they retreat when they are stressed, it's not a good idea to use an e-collar. Rather, that dog should be given plenty of positive things when in proximity to the things that cause them to fear. They should not be coddled but reinforced for outgoing behaviors. Some might read this and think that I'm suggesting that it's never helpful to use a tool like an e-collar on a fearful dog, and that is not the case.

. . .

WHERE MIGHT an e-collar be helpful with a fearful dog? E-collar training can be great for dogs who overgeneralize fear. Many of the dogs that I work with have been deemed to be fearful when in reality, they used to be fearful and now are arrogant. These dogs start out with the classic shy behavior, then transition to threatening when they feel the smallest amount of fear or stress. These dogs go from being timid of new people or dogs to full-on freak out session the moment they see a new person or dog. Explain to me how a dog is fearful if they walk down the street and lunge, bark, and growl? Certainly, they could have started out as fearful dogs, but those days are long gone. Bringing attention to yourself is not a smart method of self-preservation.

WHAT THESE DOGS now need is to understand that threatening other people or dogs that are not even paying attention to them is excessive and will not be tolerated. I don't find that these dogs thrive with 100% positive methods, because they gain so much confidence every time they use their reactive side to get what they want. Remember that every time your dog barks, growls, or lunges at a person or dog, and that person moves away from them, your dog convinces themselves that they scared that person away. That confidence transforms itself in most dogs very quickly, and thus the reason for needing an e-collar, but a prong collar can also be a good solution. When the dog is no longer making intimidating threats, then focus on your positive rein-forcement training.

IF YOUR DOG is truly fearful, don't use correction on them, use patience and plenty of positive scenarios to bring them out of their shell. If they are being a threatening jerk, you can read more about this topic in the next book that I am writing on the topic of using the e-collar to solve aggression issues.

*PLACE **command***

As a dog trainer, I find great joy in not wasting people's time by training their dog to do useless things. Many trainers have a standard syllabus that they tackle with every single dog that they work with. For myself, I don't have such a game plan. I only address the issues that clients are having, so, I rarely train their dogs to do anything that they don't specifically ask me to help with. Place is like a command that 90% of clients have already taught their dogs to some degree. Most clients have taught their dogs to go to bed, but they struggle to have their dog stay on the bed when there is a distraction. Place is just the remedy for that issue. Place means to go to bed and do not leave the bed until I tell you that you can get off the bed. I joke with my clients when teaching this command that in a week or two of training, their dog will be capable of staying on the bed if a marching band comes into your home.

I TEACH the place command to every client for four reasons;

1. IT'S the best way of reinforcing the four pillars of e-collar training (Where the stimulation is coming from, how to turn it on, how to turn it off, and how to avoid the stimulation entirely)

2. It's a very useable command that all of my clients will use on a daily basis

3. It's great for showing your dog that the e-collar can be used when the dog is close to us, or farther away from us

4. I like teaching the dog to go away from us, directly after teaching them to come to us

I TEACH it on the 2nd session with the client, so the client's dog will now have seven days of understanding the 4 pillars of e-collar training before starting place training. The clients will now have a command that they can use when cooking dinner so that the dog will not be walking around the kitchen trying to steal food or begging at the table.

. . .

IF YOUR DOG already knows a command like go to bed, you can continue to use it, but remember that you will continue to have low expectations surrounding your go to bed command. If your dog gets up after a few minutes, no big deal. However, when you give a place command, it's not negotiable.

TO START YOUR TRAINING, you'll need a bag full of tasty treats, your dog's bed, a leash, and your e-collar. Walk your dog over to the bed, and don't give them any commands. Just use a treat to incentivize them to go onto the bed. When they are on the bed, say good boy or good girl and then tell them they can get off the bed and give them another treat. This is clearly the easiest part of the training. After about 10 repetitions, start to say Place about 2-3 feet away from the place, as you incentivize them to go on. Most dogs will come off the bed to get the treat and then go right back on the bed, hoping for another treat. Your dog will learn the word place with repetition, it usually takes 2-3 days.

WHEN YOUR DOG is confident doing this, end the lesson and let your dog rest. Later that day, start another session by putting your e-collar on and setting it to the lowest level your dog will feel. Tell your dog to place, and incentivize them to go to the bed with a treat in your hand then tell them good and give them the treat when they get onto the bed. Ask them to sit, and tell them good, and give them a calm pat on the head, then drop your leash and walk away from them about 4-6 feet. Most dogs will choose to follow their owners, at which point you will hold down the continuous button on your e-collar. Pick up the leash and help your dog back to the bed, then release the button. If it takes you a few moments to get them back on, that's ok, there is no rush. Praise your dog calmly for going back to the bed and then drop the leash again and walk away from the bed. If your dog follows you again (which most will) then hold down the button again, pick up the leash and walk them back to the bed and then release the button. Do this until your dog shows you that they are starting to understand. There are two classic signs that I look for when training dogs to do place and almost every one of the 1500+ dogs that I have taught place will give you one or both of these signs when they are starting to understand what is expected of them.

1. THEY WILL START to run back to the bed on their own in hopes of turning off the e-collar stimulation

2. They will move their head just a few inches like they are going to leave the bed, but stop themselves from leaving the bed on their own

WHEN YOU NOTICE one or both of these signs, it's time to slightly increase the level on your e-collar. This is one of those scenarios in which I really like to have an e-collar with 100 or more levels. If your e-collar only goes from 1-10, an increase from a level 2 to a level 3 will likely be too much. If your e-collar has 100 levels, increase 1-3 levels at a time for each time your dog leaves the bed, until you find a sufficient number. A sufficient number will keep your dog from leaving the bed when you walk away. End the session when you can walk away from them about 10-15 feet without them leaving.

FOR YOUR NEXT LESSON, start where you left off. In this lesson, the goal is to start adding distractions. Don't start at the highest level that you were using in the last lesson, rather start again at your lowest level and increase again until you find a good level. Now you'll want to start adding distractions. Drop the leash and walk away from the bed. Get one of your dog's toys and bounce it or throw it, open and close your refrigerator, etc. You will need to increase your e-collar level as the distraction increases, so again, increase by 1-3 levels until your dog responds accordingly. When your dog is thriving at the place, ring the doorbell and open and close the front door. Two 5-15 minute sessions daily are what I suggest for 2 weeks.

REMEMBER to only give the place command when you have the e-collar on, if you don't, your dog will learn that they can ignore your command without any consequences. If a neighbor unexpectedly knocks on your door and your dog is not wearing the e-collar, you can either put your dog in a spare room for a few moments or lock the door, put your e-collar on your dog and use the scenario for training purposes.

DON'T I need to say stay? Is a question that I get daily. Stay in implied within the place command. Place means to go to the bed, good means keep doing what you are doing, and OK, YES, or FREE means you are done and can come off.

STOP excessive barking when visitors come to the door

For many years I taught my clients that they should have their dogs go to the bed when visitors come to the door. After teaching about 1000 clients the place command, I decided to soften my approach. Now I give clients two options, they can either have their dog stay on the bed, or they can allow their dogs the ability to greet visitors if they wish. Both options come with inherent problems. When you have an overwhelmingly social dog stay on the bed, they often will start to whine or bark. This can be addressed, or it can be avoided by not making the dog stay on the bed in the first place. Many of my clients want their dogs to stay on the bed because they are concerned that their dog will jump on visitors. In this case, I suggest that they allow the dog the ability to greet visitors, and then we fix the jumping issue, that issue is covered in the next chapter.

IF YOU WANT your dog to stay on the bed because they are aggressive towards people coming to your home, the place command can be helpful. If your dog starts to bark while on the bed, allow your dog 7 days of training on the place and then you can address the issue. Why wait 7 days to stop the barking? Your dog now knows the rules of the place and will stay on the bed reliably. It's counterproductive to start using the e-collar too quickly to stop barking if they are barking while on the place because they can get confused. After your dog is doing well with the place, have them on the place when a visitor comes over. I like to allow about 7 barks because it's natural for dogs to bark when a visitor comes to their home. If they don't stop on their own, say (No More Barking) then wait about one second. If they don't stop barking, hold down the continuous button until they stop barking, and then release the button. Start at a low level and increase by 1-3 levels as needed to rectify the issue.

Stopping dogs from jumping when visitors come to your home

Dogs jumping on visitors is about as common as our cold winters here in Canada, but now to worry because it's very easy to stop with your e-collar. Start by putting your e-collar on and invite a visitor to come to your home. When they arrive, your dog should get excited and start to jump on them. No need to say anything when they jump, just start at a nice low e-collar level and hold down the continuous button until they get down. If you find that that the e-collar level is not affecting them at all, slowly increase your level by 1-3 levels until they stop jumping. When they get down, your visitors can calmly give them attention when four paws are on the ground. If they want to give your dog a treat or two, have them drop the treats on the ground instead of giving your dog a treat from their hand. Treats in a person's hand can inspire some dogs to jump again, especially small dogs so it's better to drop them on the ground. That's it, I told you it was easy. Be careful to not use an excessively high level when using this protocol as it could make your dog apprehensive about greeting visitors. Take your time and your dog will be a patient greeter in no time.

. . .

As MENTIONED in the chapter on place training, if a neighbor unexpectedly knocks on your door and your dog is not wearing the e-collar, you can either put your dog in a spare room for a few moments or lock the door, put your e-collar on your dog and use the scenario for training purposes.

So WHY DID I suggest not using a command to stop jumping and then suggest using a command to stop jumping? The simple answer is that we are not allowing any jumping, but we are allowing some barking, and so we must have some sort of a verbal cue.

MANGO DOGS IS GROWING and we'll help you get up to speed on your dog training skills, handle all of your marketing and you'll be part of our team. For more information go to: www.mangodogs.com/join

.

FAQ PART 5

*B**arking at the window***
If I had to guess how many of my client's dogs excessively bark at the window I would say about 95% of my client's dogs have this issue. They do it because it makes them feel good about themselves, but it can be annoying for us humans. Think about it for a moment, they bark, the dog or person across the street walks away every time, and your dog convinces themself that they scared them off.

BEFORE STARTING you'll want to decide if you want to allow some barking at the window or no barking. If you want your dog to bark when you are not home, you are going to use a command like (No More Barking). If you have tenants downstairs who hate when your dog barks, you will not be using a command. To address the issue, wait until your dog starts barking at the window and then say (No More Barking), if they do not stop, hold down the continuous button on your e-collar, starting at a low level. If they continue, increase the level by 1-3 levels until they have stopped barking then release the button. If you don't want your dog to bark at all at the window, just omit the command and you might want to look into buying a bark collar to solve that issue when you are not home.

Do you ever use bark collars?

My clients rarely use bark collar, however, there are some scenarios in which they can be very helpful. If you are about to get kicked out of your apartment because your dog is barking when you are at work, get yourself a bark collar ASAP. Bark collars will give a correction when your dog barks, which stops them from barking. Spray collars work on a similar principle, however, they spray the dog's neck with compressed air or a citronella scent that some dogs don't like the smell of. I tend to stay away from spray collars as I find they rarely work. Bark collars are much more effective, but you'll want to buy the right one. Models by Dogtra, Garmin, and E-Collar technologies are the best I've seen. The main consideration you will need to make before buying a bark collar will be to know that most bark collars are only useful for single dog homes. Most bark collars have an audible sensor on them that detects the sound of a dog bark which triggers the tone, vibrate, or correction. If you have more than one dog, you'll need to find a bark collar that only triggers based on vibration sensing. Vibration sensing bark collars are only triggered when the collars sensor senses a strong vibration from your dog's vocal cords, then triggering the bark collar.

My dog chases my cats in the house, can I use the e-collar?

Having a harmonious household with dogs and cats living amongst each other can be a thing of beauty, but it can also be very challenging. If your dog wants to kill your cat, this section is not going to cover such issues, for that, I would highly suggest that you call in a professional dog trainer to help you navigate those waters safely. If like many of my clients, your dog loves chasing their cats for fun, this section should help you find some peace and quiet. As with everything else in this book, you should have finished your foundation training before starting this part of your training.

· · ·

YOU'LL WANT to choose a cue that will stop your dog from chasing your cat/cats, I suggest something simple like Enough Roughhousing. You'll want to remember that your e-collar will need to be on your dog a lot if your dog has this issue because if you allow them to chase your cat 50% of the day without any consequences, they will never get tired of challenging you when you ask them to stop. Wait for your dog to start chasing your cat, and then give your command, hold down your continuous stimulation button on your e-collar and release when your dog stops chasing the cat/cats. Start at a nice low level and slowly increase the level as needed to get your dog to stop. That's it, easy stuff. I've helped roughly 500-600 clients with this issue and it's just that simple.

THE TWO DIFFERENT *styles of e-collar training*

Each trainer has their own way to use the e-collar. Some are devoted to the momentary stimulation mode, others are staunch continuous advocates. Some never use the tone and others use it often. The following is not a declaration of which ways are better because, in reality, they both work.

THE STYLE that I was taught many years ago by my mentor is hands down the most commonly used method in e-collar training today. Because this method has never been given a name, I will refer to it as the tapping method. In this method, the trainer conditions the dog to the e-collar by selecting the lowest level they can see the dog responding to, then tapping the momentary button while giving the dog a command like come, or sit. The dog is then given a treat. The idea behind this method ultimately that the dog will learn to like the stimulation and also learn that the stimulation is coming from the dog's owner or trainer. After about a week of training, the dog trainer will then start to increase the level if the dog is not doing something they are being asked to do. In this method, tone or vibration are not used ever. Some trainers tap, tap, tap the continuous button and others will transition into the continuous stimulation, this seems to be personal preference. In essence, a low stimulation will indicate that the dog trainer is asking them to do something, and a higher level is indicating that they ignored the command and now have to deal with a more annoying feeling.

I used the above method for many years and trained about 1100 dogs with this method and it's a fine method but I changed my style about 4 years ago because I was unhappy with how 5% of my client's dogs were responding during the e-collar conditioning period. In 5% of dogs, the treats they were being given were not enough of an incentive to get them over the tiny negative feeling of the e-collar at a low level. In fairness, it wasn't brutal training, these dogs had e-collar with at least 100 level capability, and many of them were working at incredibly low levels like 2-5/100, yet, some of them looked unhappy for the first few sessions even with yummy treats. This caused me to play around with my methods in hopes that I could create an even more fun e-collar conditioning teaching protocol.

The next style is the style that you were reading about earlier in this book, let's call it the tone method. In this method of conditioning, the trainer asks the dog to come to them and then directly after will tap the tone button on the e-collar. This tone is used to communicate with the dog a few things. Firstly it helps the dog understand that the tone is connected to you because they hear it directly after your command. Secondly, it's used to tell the dog that you want them to come back to you and get a treat, think of it as a clicker. The tone seems to be less offensive than the low-level momentary stimulation used in the previous method we discussed which is why I prefer it. It's also important to note that this tone method is done outside when most trainers who use the previous method teach their conditioning inside. I prefer teaching outside because the smells outside help any sensitive dogs focus less on the e-collar training which also produces less stress.

· · ·

THE TONE METHOD is less stress-inducing, but it's also something that you should not use if your dog has used an invisible fence before. These dogs are always leery of electric collars, and they associate the beep to mean that they are close to a line that should not be crossed. If you have such a dog, you have a few options you can use no tone at all, and just use your come command or you can use the vibration in place of the tone.

SURELY BOTH METHODS WORK WELL, but I prefer the tone method because I find that my clients are more consistent with this method. Hundreds of times, I've watched clients not press the button when I used to use the tapping method. They felt bad that they had to tap the momentary button even if the stimulation was at a very low level. The tone method addresses this issue because the dog never feels the stimulation unless they completely ignore our verbal and tone command. So why use the tone, when we can just use a verbal command? The tone sound comes from the collar, this is important because if your dog is far away from you, they will always hear that tone, and that means that we never have to ask ourselves if our dog even heard our command.

TRAINING *two or more dogs at the same time*

One of the most frequent questions that I get from readers of this book is based around training multiple dogs with e-collars and I often train with clients who own 2 or more dogs. When I take on such a client, we set the client up with a 2 or 3 dog e-collar model like the EZ902 or EZ903 from E-Collar Technologies. Sometimes the client wants to save money by only purchasing a one dog unit, and trying to use it on all of their dogs, but this thriftiness will not pay off. If you currently have one dog and are considering getting another, be sure to buy an e-collar that you can expand to a multiple dog device.

. . .

YOU'LL HAVE to start your e-collar training individually with your dogs. After a few short weeks, this individual training time will end and you can work with 2 or more of your dogs at the same time, so please be patient until then. I'm privy to know most of the world's best e-collar trainers personally, and I don't know one of them who is capable of training multiple dogs at the same time, on day one. Each day you will go about your training homework instructed in this book until you get all of your dogs well-trained off-leash individually. It goes without saying that if you have 3 or more dogs, you would start them individually, then two dogs at a time then three, etc. When training the place command, you can do two dogs at the same time, but again, not on day one, wait until all of your dogs are advanced at the place command before integrating the other dog/dogs.

ONE THING TO note when training 2 or more dogs at the same time is that you cannot press 2 buttons at the same time. No e-collar on the market is capable of stimulating two collars at the same time, and this is rarely something that dog owners even realize. That means that you have to tap one button, and then tap the next button. When you tap or hold both buttons at the same time, the signal will quit and neither collar will get the stimulation. When working on recall with multiple dog homes, I always remind my clients that in most multiple dog homes, there is going to be one dog who leads the charge, especially in homes with just 2 dogs. One dog is always running off and needs more attention, and the other dog tends to follow that dog if they come back. When this is the case focus your efforts on the trouble-making dog, as the easier dog will fall in line when they see their role model doing so.

IF YOU HAVE multiple dogs in the same home that are fighting, I highly recommend contacting a qualified dog trainer who can help you pasted these issues. Such cases I do not feel comfortable writing about, because there is so much that can go wrong if the process is not done perfectly. Without giving you a process, I will say that having a 2 or 3 dog units for such cases is not ideal. Rather I have my clients buy 2 different e-collars so that if they need to, they can correct both or all of their dogs at the same time without having to tap one button, then another button. When a dog fight breaks out, every split second counts. To that point, don't waste your money on small capacity e-collars when you have two or more dogs fighting in the same. I prefer something like the EZ900 with upgraded RX120 collar. You would need two units so you can call the company and get them to upgrade the collar, and also change the plastic skins on one of the remotes so that you know which remote is for which dog. When a potential client calls me on the phone, I tell them over the phone that their e-collars alone are going to cost them at least $600 because I only use the best e-collars, and we will have to buy multiple units to do the job properly. Don't cheap out if your dogs are fighting, it could cost one of your dogs their life, and don't put your hands into a fight, that is the fastest way to end up in the hospital. My computer hard drive is full of photos of dog trainers and dog owners who were almost killed by their dogs after a fight started. Keep your dogs away from each other until you can get a quality trainer to help you.

CHECK **out your (2) free step by step e-collar training video series at www.tedsbooks.com/watch**

THANK YOU!

If you have questions, feel free to email me personally, I love helping out dog owners and trainers. Email: ted@tedsbooks.com.

DON'T FORGET **to review the book on Amazon, it really helps me out!!! Thanks in advance.**

Ted Efthymiadis

- *Join the mailing list*
- *Find all of my other books*
- *Watch your 2 free video series!*
- *Access online training sessions with me*
- *Buy my aggressive dog training DVD's*
- *At www.tedsbooks.com*

ALSO BY TED EFTHYMIADIS

All titles are available on Amazon in Kindle and Physical book some, some are available in audiobook version from www.audible.com

Giving Up On My Dog: A straightforward directive for those close to giving up on their dog

Prong Collar Training for Pet Dogs: The only resource you'll need to train your pet dog with the aid of a prong collar (Dog Training for Pet Dogs) (Volume 1)

Potty Training Puppy: A comprehensive guide to help you navigate the crappy job of house training your puppy

Thriving Dog Trainers: An indispensable tool to help you start or repair your dog training business (Business books for dog trainers)

Thriving Dog Trainers Book 2: Get better clients, work less, enjoy your life and business (Business books for dog trainers)

Made in the USA
Las Vegas, NV
17 March 2022